# BIOGRAPHIC
# MARILYN

# BIOGRAPHIC
# MARILYN

**KATIE GREENWOOD**

**ILLUSTRATED BY
MATT CARR**

AMMONITE
PRESS

First published 2019 by
Ammonite Press
an imprint of Guild of Master Craftsman Publications Ltd
Castle Place, 166 High Street, Lewes, East Sussex, BN7 1XU,
United Kingdom
www.ammonitepress.com

ISBN 978 1 78145 370 4

Publisher: Jason Hook
Concept Design: Matt Carr
Design & Illustration: Matt Carr & Robin Shields
Editor: Jamie Pumfrey

Colour reproduction by GMC Reprographics
Printed and bound in Turkey

# CONTENTS

# ICONOGRAPHIC

WHEN WE CAN RECOGNIZE AN ACTOR BY
A SET OF ICONS, WE CAN ALSO RECOGNIZE
HOW COMPLETELY THAT ACTOR AND
THEIR WORK HAVE ENTERED OUR
CULTURE AND OUR CONSCIOUSNESS.

# INTRODUCTION

Marilyn Monroe represents the epitome of 1950s Hollywood glamour and was the foremost sex symbol of her day. Her public image embraced a potent mix of wide-eyed innocence and desirability, symbolizing "every man's love affair with America," as Norman Mailer once commented, as well as a wider shift in attitudes towards female sexuality. Marilyn's rise to an unprecedented level of fame went hand in hand with a mass media boom, helping to cement her status as the ultimate post-war icon.

Gorgeous, charming, witty and generous, Marilyn often wore her heart on her sleeve. When nude calendar photos resurfaced just as her career hit the big time (taken when she was an aspiring starlet and reappearing in the first issue of *Playboy* magazine in 1953), her studio Twentieth Century Fox wanted her to deny posing for the pictures. She didn't. Instead, Marilyn admitted that she had needed the money to survive hard times. Her honesty won the hearts of her fans and helped to further endear her to a truly global audience.

Privately, Marilyn found it increasingly difficult to integrate her public persona with her own self-image. Growing up had not been easy – having both an absent father and mentally unstable mother led to a traumatic cycle of foster care, with the associated feelings of rejection and a deep desire for approval spilling over into all aspects of her life. To escape her insecurities and the pressures of fame, she turned to sedatives – more specifically barbiturates – to cope. At first these helped Marilyn to sleep and calm her bouts of anxiety, but they led her into a downward spiral of dependency and erratic behaviour, and ultimately to a tragically young death.

"I'M A FAILURE AS A WOMAN. MY MEN EXPECT SO MUCH OF ME, BECAUSE OF THE IMAGE THEY'VE MADE OF ME – AND THAT I'VE MADE OF MYSELF – AS A SEX SYMBOL... THEY EXPECT BELLS TO RING AND WHISTLES TO WHISTLE, BUT MY ANATOMY IS THE SAME AS ANY OTHER WOMAN'S AND I CAN'T LIVE UP TO IT."

—Marilyn Monroe, *Marilyn: The Last Take* by Peter Harry Brown and Patte B. Barham, 1992

It would be wrong to depict Marilyn purely as a victim. In a world where women were expected be sexy or smart, but rarely both, the beautiful and intelligent Monroe – who read widely, admired art and wrote poetry – became frustrated with being typecast as the ultimate 'dumb blonde'. After going on strike against her studio, she formed her own production company in order to pursue multi-dimensional roles with greater financial reward. It was not the first time she had gone against the accepted workings of the Hollywood studio system – Marilyn's early career is littered with tales of her fending off predatory male attention, stories of great relevance today.

Marilyn became a living legend, not least because of her talent as an actress and the luminosity of her screen presence. Her tragic death at the age of 36 helped to ensure her legacy. She came to personify both the allure of superstardom and the negative consequences of a life lived under the relentless glare of the spotlight. People continue to be fascinated by the seeming paradoxes that her life embodied: fragility and strength, innocence and sexuality, vulnerability and power.

"MARILYN HAS THE FRAGILITY OF A FEMALE BUT THE CONSTITUTION OF AN OX. SHE IS A BEAUTIFUL HUMMINGBIRD MADE OF IRON. HER ONLY TROUBLE IS THAT SHE IS A VERY PURE PERSON IN A VERY IMPURE WORLD."

—Paula Strasberg, from *The Many Lives of Marilyn Monroe* by Sarah Churchwell, 2004

# MARILYN MONROE

## 01
## LIFE

"TO HAVE SURVIVED, SHE WOULD HAVE HAD TO BE EITHER MORE CYNICAL OR EVEN FURTHER FROM REALITY THAN SHE WAS. INSTEAD, SHE WAS A POET ON A STREET CORNER TRYING TO RECITE TO A CROWD PULLING AT HER CLOTHES."

—Arthur Miller, *Timebends: A Life*, 1987

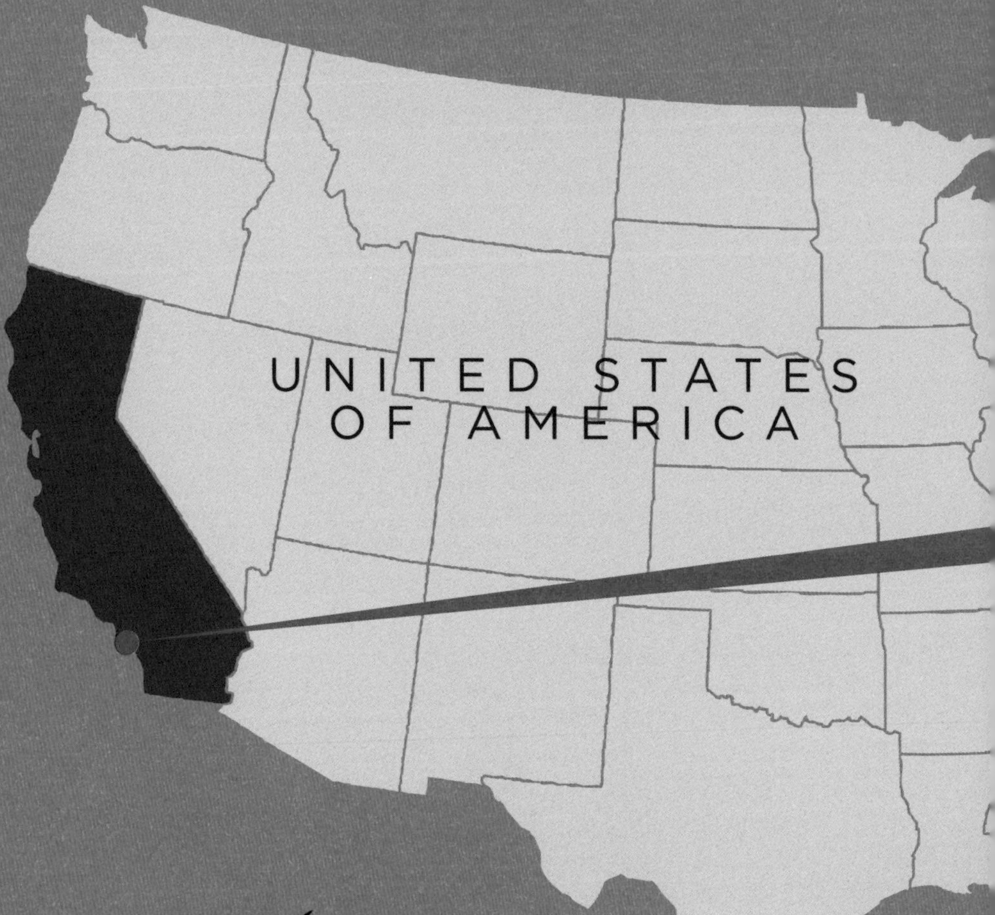

UNITED STATES
OF AMERICA

◀ Born in the same year:
**Harper Lee** (1926–2016),
American novelist. Marilyn
was reading Lee's novel
*To Kill a Mockingbird* at
the time of her death.

# MARILYN MONROE

**was born on 1 June 1926 in Los Angeles, California, USA**

Norma Jeane Mortenson (later Marilyn Monroe) was born in the charity ward of the Los Angeles General Hospital. By the time of her birth, Los Angeles had already become the centre of the world's film industry – in 1910 Hollywood was incorporated as a district and by 1921 around 80 per cent of the world's film industry was based there. Marilyn's mother, Gladys, worked as a film cutter for Consolidated Film Industries, a company that processed the reels coming out of the studios. However, Gladys's mental and financial instability meant that she was unable to care for her daughter through much of Marilyn's childhood, leaving her to be raised by a series of family and friends. Marilyn would never know her real father.

# HOLLYWOOD

# 1926 IN FILM

The world of cinema was in a state of transition when Marilyn was born. Experiments in sound culminated in the release of the first feature-length 'talkie', *The Jazz Singer*, the following year. The musical famously marked the decline of the silent era, and the beginning of Hollywood's Golden Age.

## DON JUAN

is the first feature film to have a synchronized soundtrack (but no dialogue) using Warner Brothers' new Vitaphone system.

Alfred Hitchcock's second feature

## THE MOUNTAIN EAGLE

is screened to producers, it is postponed to the following year. Today no prints of the film are known to exist and it is considered lost.

## AL JOLSON

sings three songs wearing blackface in the Warner Brothers Vitaphone short, *A Plantation Act* – a test film for *The Jazz Singer*.

Silent screen idol

## RUDOLPH VALENTINO

dies at 31. His funeral is held in New York and is attended by 100,000 people.

Actress Clara Bow refuses to sign the standard 'morality' clause in her contract with Paramount, which was aimed at preventing scandal.

ADMIT ONE ADMIT ONE

In Germany, the earliest surviving animated feature **THE ADVENTURES OF PRINCE ACHMED** is released.

An optical sound-on-film system called

# MOVIETONE

(vs. the synchronized sound-on-disc system of Vitaphone) is developed for the Fox Film Corporation.

# GRETA GARBO

stars in *The Flesh and the Devil*, marking the start of her romance with co-star John Gilbert.

___

## ADMIT ONE

The silent blockbuster *The Black Pirate* is the first feature-length colour film, produced by and starring

# DOUGLAS FAIRBANKS

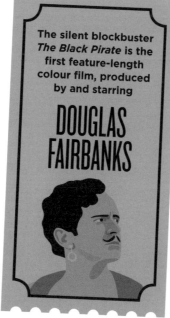

Sergei Eisenstein's Soviet propaganda film

# BATTLESHIP POTEMKIN

premieres in the US. It is notable for its use of innovative montage editing techniques.

 A review of

# MOANA

a semi-fictional film about traditional Polynesian life uses the word 'documentary' for the first time.

# MARILYN'S FAMILY TREE

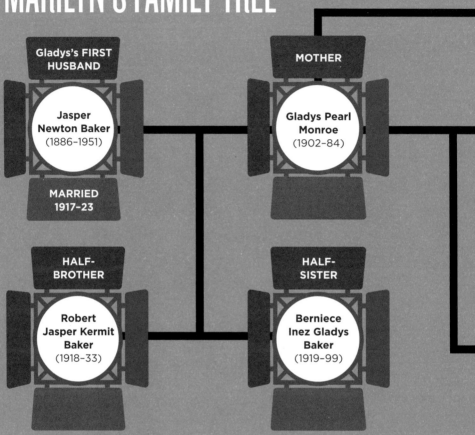

**Gladys's FIRST HUSBAND**

Jasper Newton Baker (1886–1951)

**MARRIED 1917–23**

**MOTHER**

Gladys Pearl Monroe (1902–84)

**HALF-BROTHER**

Robert Jasper Kermit Baker (1918–33)

**HALF-SISTER**

Berniece Inez Gladys Baker (1919–99)

Half of Marilyn's family tree is missing – who her father was remains unclear. Her birth certificate lists Edward Mortensen, the man married to but separated from her mother at the time she was born. Speculation has pinpointed a range of other candidates, the most likely being Gladys's colleague Charles Stanley Gifford. However, he refused to acknowledge or even meet Marilyn. On the maternal side of her family is a history of mental illness – grandmother Della Mae was institutionalized at the age of 51, dying soon afterwards when Marilyn was just one year old. Her great-grandfather hung himself when she was seven and her mother was diagnosed with paranoid schizophrenia in 1934, when she was eight. Though she had half-siblings from Gladys's previous marriage, she was unaware of them for some time and would meet her half-sister Berniece only a handful of times (her half-brother Robert had died at the age of 15). Marilyn yearned for a family of her own, but she would suffer a series of miscarriages and was never able to have children.

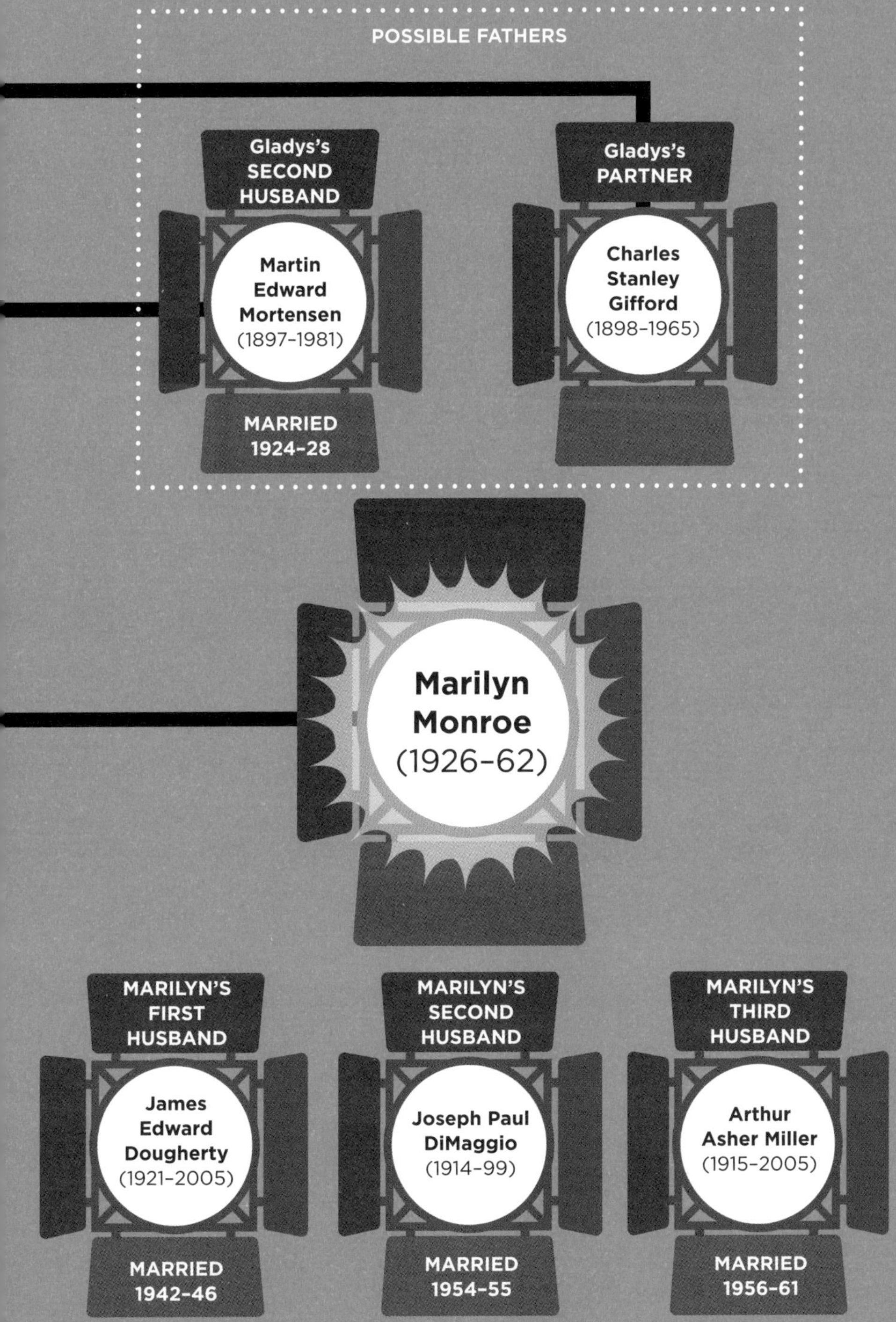

POSSIBLE FATHERS

Gladys's
SECOND
HUSBAND

Martin
Edward
Mortensen
(1897–1981)

MARRIED
1924–28

Gladys's
PARTNER

Charles
Stanley
Gifford
(1898–1965)

Marilyn
Monroe
(1926–62)

MARILYN'S
FIRST
HUSBAND

James
Edward
Dougherty
(1921–2005)

MARRIED
1942–46

MARILYN'S
SECOND
HUSBAND

Joseph Paul
DiMaggio
(1914–99)

MARRIED
1954–55

MARILYN'S
THIRD
HUSBAND

Arthur
Asher Miller
(1915–2005)

MARRIED
1956–61

# WHAT'S IN A NAME?

Norma Jeane became Marilyn Monroe in 1946 – a name credited to film studio executive Ben Lyon – though she would not legally change it until 1956. Like her idol Jean Harlow, she acted under her mother's maiden name, and sometimes used pseudonyms to preserve her privacy. Here are some of the names – official and unofficial – that she was known by during her life and career.

**BORN**

## NORMA JEANE MORTENSON

On her birth certificate Marilyn's name differs from her listed father, Edward Mortensen, by one letter.

**FIRST MARRIAGE**

## NORMA JEANE DOUGHERTY

**BAPTISED**

## NORMA JEANE BAKER

CHILDHOOD NICKNAME: **The Mouse**

BY COLUMNIST HEDDA HOPPER: **The Blowtorch Blonde**

AS A PSYCHIATRIC PATIENT: **Faye Miller**

AS A HOTEL GUEST: **Zelda Zonk**

1925 1930 1935 1940

Life & death   Career   Love life   Unofficial names

MODEL
JEAN NORMAN/
MONA MONROE

SECOND
MARRIAGE
MARILYN
DIMAGGIO

THIRD
MARRIAGE
MARILYN
MILLER

ACTRESS
MARILYN
MONROE

DIED
MARILYN
MONROE

1945   1950   1955   1960

LIFE

21

# A BROKEN HOME LIFE

> "WHEN I WAS A KID, THE WORLD OFTEN SEEMED A PRETTY GRIM PLACE. I LOVED TO ESCAPE THROUGH GAMES AND MAKE-BELIEVE. YOU CAN DO THAT EVEN BETTER AS AN ACTRESS, BUT SOMETIMES IT SEEMS LIKE YOU ESCAPE ALTOGETHER AND PEOPLE NEVER LET YOU COME BACK."

—Marilyn Monroe

## 1935

Gladys suffers a breakdown and is institutionalized with schizophrenia. Gladys's best friend, Grace McKee, organizes Marilyn's care and applies to become her legal guardian. Grace will be instrumental in encouraging Marilyn to become a movie star – her own unrealized ambition.

## 1933

Gladys moves temporarily into the Bolender home, before taking out a loan to buy a house for her and her daughter. They move in together in the autumn. Gladys rents out rooms in the house to an English couple, George and Maude Atkinson, to help pay the bills.

## 1926

Born at Los Angeles General Hospital. She stays with her mother Gladys for 12 days, before the financial pressure of single motherhood leads to Marilyn being placed with her first foster family – Ida and Wayne Bolender – on 13 June. The Bolenders are strict and ultra-religious. She will see her mother only intermittently during her early childhood.

> "THIS SAD, BITTER CHILD WHO GREW UP TOO FAST IS HARDLY EVER OUT OF MY HEART. WITH SUCCESS ALL AROUND ME, I CAN STILL FEEL HER FRIGHTENED EYES LOOKING OUT OF MINE."

—Marilyn Monroe

**1935** Marilyn is placed with the Giffen family, who offer to adopt her. Gladys refuses, and Marilyn stays with her maternal grandmother for a period. Grace becomes Marilyn's legal guardian on 1 June, but she is unable to care for her and takes Marilyn to the Los Angeles County Orphanage on 13 September. Gladys visits Marilyn and takes her to the movies throughout her stay.

**1942** Unable to care for her and not wanting to send her back to the orphanage, Grace arranges for Marilyn to marry Jim Dougherty, literally the boy-next-door. Marilyn and Jim marry on 19 June, shortly after her 16th birthday.

**1939** Enid and Sam Knebelcamp become her foster family for a short time.

**1936** Grace takes Marilyn out of the orphanage and Marilyn stays with her and her new husband, Doc Goddard, for a while. The following year she is placed with Ida Martin, Marilyn's great-aunt by marriage, who she stays with until August 1938.

**1938** Marilyn lives with the Goddards and then with Grace's aunt, Ana Lower, in November. Ana becomes the most stable influence in Marilyn's life, and Marilyn spends the majority of her time living with Ana from this point. However, suffering a heart condition, Ana is not always able to look after her, and Marilyn will shuttle between various homes throughout the rest of her childhood.

# MARILYN LIVED IN AT LEAST 43 HOMES IN HER 36 YEARS

**KEY**

- House
- Orphanage
- Hotel

Marilyn had nine different childhood homes – but she lived with her mother in just two of them. Other addresses included those of her foster parents and a legal guardian, and an orphanage. These experiences set a precedent for a life spent on the move, including several extended hotel stays.

**Marilyn only ever owned one home – bought six months before she died**

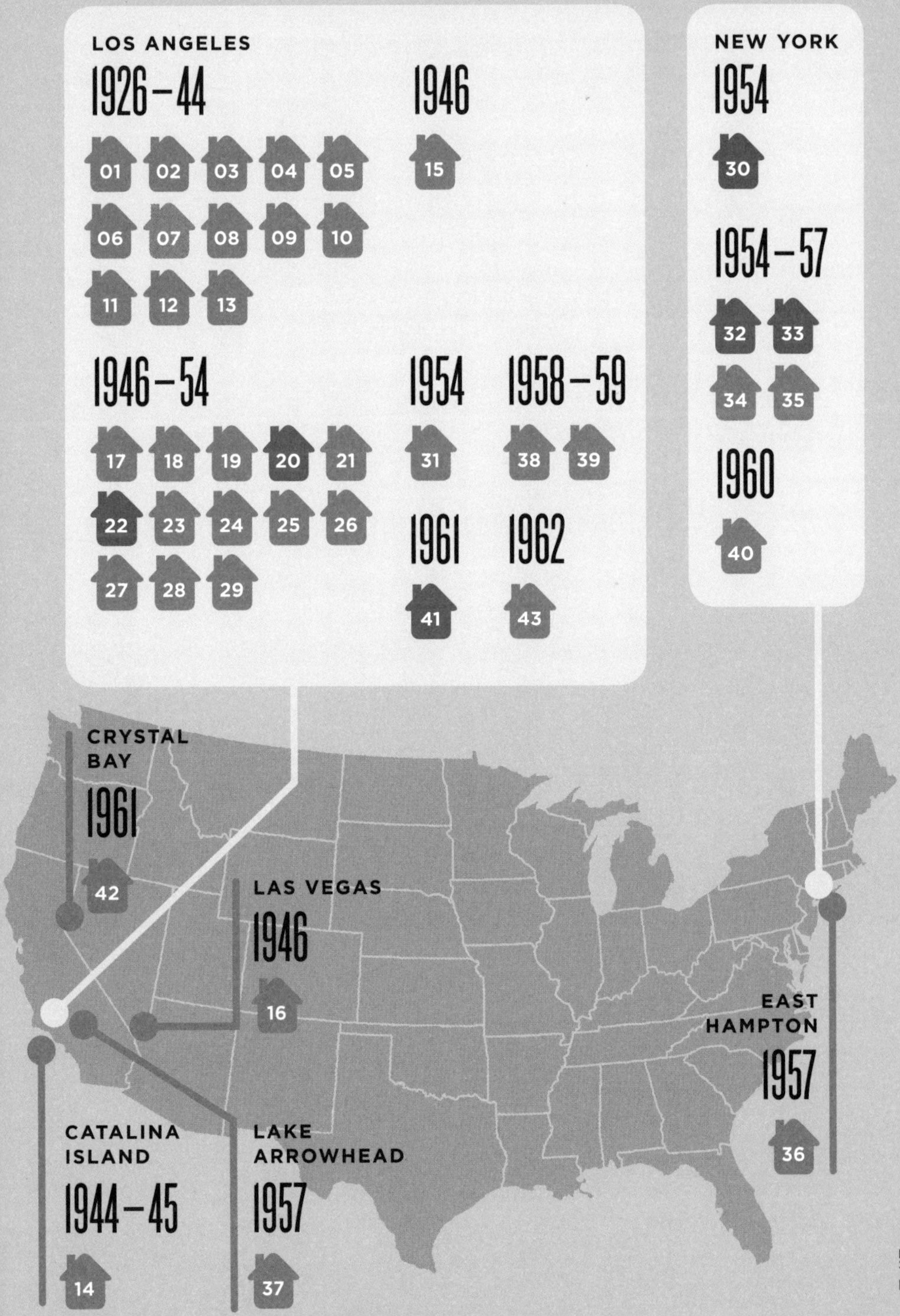

**LOS ANGELES**

**1926–44**

01 02 03 04 05
06 07 08 09 10
11 12 13

**1946**

15

**1946–54**

17 18 19 20 21
22 23 24 25 26
27 28 29

**1954**

31

**1958–59**

38 39

**1961**

41

**1962**

43

**NEW YORK**

**1954**

30

**1954–57**

32 33
34 35

**1960**

40

**CRYSTAL BAY**

**1961**

42

**LAS VEGAS**

**1946**

16

**EAST HAMPTON**

**1957**

36

**CATALINA ISLAND**

**1944–45**

14

**LAKE ARROWHEAD**

**1957**

37

# THE WALK TO FAME

**1948**

Meets mogul Joseph Schenck in February, leading to a six-month contract with Columbia, which is not renewed.

Appears on screen in two films including *Ladies of the Chorus*, where she is given a solo song and dance number.

Meets agent Johnny Hyde on New Year's Eve.

**1949**

Poses nude for a calendar, photographed by Tom Kelley, in July.

Signs a contract with MGM for her breakthrough role in John Huston's *The Asphalt Jungle* in October.

**1942**

Marries Jim Dougherty at the age of 16 on 19 June.

**1944**

Starts work at the Radioplane munitions factory in April, producing drones for the Second World War.

Discovered by army photographer David Conover who was taking morale-boosting images of women at work.

**1947**

Fox contract renewed in January.

Plays a minor role in *Dangerous Years* – her first big-screen appearance.

Fox contract is not renewed in August.

**1946**

Appears on the cover of *Family Circle* on 26 April – her first for a national magazine.

Performs her first screen test for Twentieth Century Fox in July, which leads to a six-month contract.

Divorces Jim Dougherty in September.

Dyes her hair blonde.

Changes her name to Marilyn Monroe.

**1945**

Joins the Blue Book Modeling Agency and quits her job at the factory.

PEROXIDE

## 1950

Appears on screen in four films: *A Ticket to Tomahawk, The Fireball, The Asphalt Jungle* and a small but important role in *All About Eve*, starring Bette Davis.

Her agent, Johnny Hyde, dies in December.

## 1951

Presents the Oscar for Sound Recording at the Academy Awards.

Signs a six-month contract with Fox, which is extended to a seven-year deal.

Appears on screen in five films: *Right Cross, Home Town Story, As Young as You Feel, Love Nest* and *Let's Make It Legal*.

Featured in *Collier's* magazine – her first national full-length article.

## 1952

First date with Joe DiMaggio in March.

Nude calendar photos resurface, receiving much attention.

Appears on her first cover for *Life* magazine, shot by Philippe Halsman, on 7 April.

Receives the role of Lorelei Lee in *Gentlemen Prefer Blonde*s on her birthday, 1 June.

Appears on screen in five films, including *Clash by Night* directed by Fritz Lang.

## 1953

*Niagara* is released on 21 January, featuring Marilyn performing the 'longest walk in cinema history' – 116 ft of film showing her walking away from camera.

Appears on screen in *Gentlemen Prefer Blondes*, co-starring with Jane Russell.

Presses her handprints into the pavement outside Grauman's Chinese Theatre on 26 May.

Stars in *How to Marry a Millionaire*, opposite Lauren Bacall and Betty Grable.

# FATHER FIGURES

After seeing a photograph of the man her mother believed was her father, Charles Stanley Gifford, Marilyn daydreamed that Clark Gable, 'The King of Hollywood', was her real daddy as the two shared a strong resemblance. She would star opposite Gable in *The Misfits*.

Marilyn met talent agent Johnny Hyde when she was 19. He was 53 and devoted the last years of his life to promoting her career. Though she felt genuine affection, she refused his offer of marriage – along with the promise of becoming a rich widow.

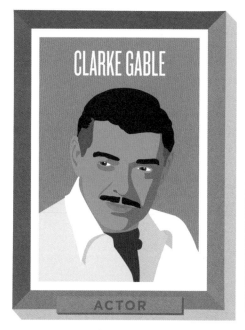

CLARKE GABLE

ACTOR

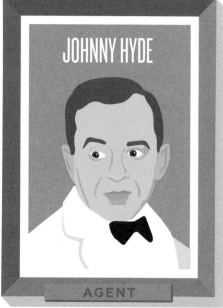

JOHNNY HYDE

AGENT

"I used to always think of him as my father, I'd pretend that he was my father. I never used to pretend that anyone was my mother, I don't know why... I was just seven years old and he was a very young man. I thought – that's how I want my father to look."

"He knew all the pain and desperate things in me. When he put his arms around me and said he loved me, I knew it was true. Nobody had ever loved me like that. I wished with all my heart I could love him back... it was like being with a whole family."

In the absence of a father, Marilyn sought out older male role models she could look up to; she admired men of intellectual prowess and seeming integrity. In her romantic relationships, she was attracted to older partners – husbands Joe DiMaggio and Arthur Miller both being more than 10 years her senior – though she often felt let down when she did not find the unconditional love she craved.

As the director of the Actors Studio in New York, Strasberg's belief in Marilyn's talent was fundamental in helping her to realize her ambition to be a serious actress. When she married Arthur Miller, Strasberg gave her away. He later spoke at her funeral.

Marilyn had written an essay on Lincoln at school and he became a childhood hero. A portrait of the president hung in pride of place in many of her homes. Later in life she became friends with Lincoln's biographer, Carl Sandburg.

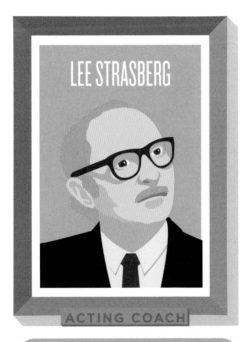

LEE STRASBERG

ACTING COACH

ABRAHAM LINCOLN

PRESIDENT

"He changed my life more than any other human being that I've met, including everyone. He helped me a great deal because he said Marilyn, you're a human being so you start with yourself."

"Most people can admire their fathers, but I never had one. I need someone to admire... My father is Abraham Lincoln... I mean I think of Lincoln as my father. He was wise and kind and good. He is my ideal, Lincoln. I love him."

# PARALLEL LIVES

More than any other actress, Marilyn looked up to Hollywood's original 'blonde bombshell' Jean Harlow. Like millions of other Americans escaping the realities of everyday life in Depression-era America, she loved to lose herself in the fantasy world of the big screen and was reportedly inconsolable when her favourite actress passed away, shortly after Marilyn's 11th birthday. In many ways, Marilyn's life would come to mirror that of her role model.

## JEAN HARLOW
## 1911 – 37

Both first married at 16

Each acted under her mother's maiden name

Both dyed their hair platinum blonde

Both loved animals

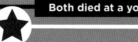

The foremost female sex symbols of their day

Both lived on North Palm Drive, Los Angeles

Went on strike against their studios to better their contracts

Both died at a young age in tragic circumstances

> "I KEPT THINKING OF HER, ROLLING THE FACTS OF HER LIFE OVER IN MY MIND... WE JUST SEEMED TO HAVE THE SAME SPIRIT OR SOMETHING, I DON'T KNOW. I KEPT WONDERING IF I WOULD DIE YOUNG LIKE HER, TOO."

—Marilyn Monroe on Jean Harlow

# MARILYN MONROE
# 1926–62

Each had 3 husbands

Each was estranged from her father

Popularly known as "blonde bombshells"

Both posed nude during their careers

Both went without underwear

Each starred opposite Clark Gable in her final film

Both became addicted to sedatives

Each attended a presidential birthday celebration shortly before her death

# MARILYN'S MEDICAL HISTORY

## EAR

Ménière's disease, a condition of the inner ear that causes dizziness, nausea and potential hearing loss, was diagnosed in 1949.

## NOSE & CHIN

X-rays have revealed that Marilyn underwent two plastic surgery operations on her nose and chin in the early days of her career.

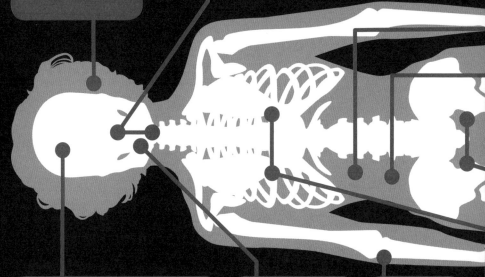

## BRAIN

Mental health issues, compounded by the effects of long-term barbiturate and alcohol addiction, led to Marilyn being admitted to a secure psychiatric ward in 1961. More than anything Marilyn feared suffering like her mother, who had been institutionalized with a diagnosis of schizophrenia when Marilyn was a little girl.

## TEETH

After having her wisdom teeth removed in 1946, Marilyn contracted trench mouth – a severe gum infection.

## SKIN

In 1946, Marilyn contracted measles.

## GALLBLADDER

Marilyn was plagued by digestive problems, and her gallbladder was removed in 1961.

## APPENDIX

Appendicitis led to an appendectomy in 1952.

MARILYN WAS **5** HOSPITALIZED TIMES

## LUNGS

She was prone to bronchitis, which led to hospitalization for the condition in 1954 and 1956. Time off from filming was attributed to severe colds – a cause that was not always believed.

## REPRODUCTIVE SYSTEM

Marilyn suffered from chronic endometriosis, a gynaecological condition where tissue akin to the lining of the womb grows outside the womb. This caused her debilitating periods and led to trouble conceiving. She underwent operations to try and relieve symptoms in 1954, 1959, 1961 and possibly in 1962.

# LA Times

# MARILYN DEAD AT 36

Eunice Murray – Marilyn's housekeeper at 12305 Fifth Helena Drive – woke at 3.00 am on 5 August with the feeling that something was wrong. Marilyn's door was locked, the light was on, but she was unresponsive. Murray quickly called psychiatrist Ralph Greenson. He arrived and broke down the door to discover Marilyn face down and naked on her bed, empty drug bottles next to her. Dr. Hyman Engelberg arrived soon after, before the police were called at 4.25 am. The levels of drugs found in the toxicology report, along with Marilyn's recent depression and previous suicide attempts, meant that her death – between 8.30 and 10.30 p.m. the previous evening – was ruled a probable suicide.

## DIED: 4 AUGUST 1962
## FUNERAL: 8 AUGUST 1962

Held at Westwood Memorial Park, Los Angeles, Marilyn's funeral was a small, private affair from which Marilyn's Hollywood friends were excluded. She was buried in her favourite green Pucci dress with a bouquet of pink roses from Joe DiMaggio.

Hugh Hefner, founder of *Playboy* magazine, is interred in the vault next to Marilyn, which he purchased in 1992 for a reported $75,000. "Spending eternity next to Marilyn is too sweet to pass up," he told the *LA Times*.

## WAS THERE A CONSPIRACY?

Many theories exist surrounding Marilyn's death, including accidental overdose rather than suicide, and murder linked to her rumoured affairs with John and Robert Kennedy. The FBI, CIA, union leader Jimmy Hoffa and mob boss Sam Giancana have all been implicated. The case was reopened in 1982 due to media speculation but resulted in no new findings.

## CAUSE OF DEATH:

**Barbiturate poisoning**
**Verdict: Probable suicide**

MARILYN

# MARILYN
# MONROE

## 02
## WORLD

"HOLLYWOOD'S A PLACE WHERE THEY'LL PAY YOU A THOUSAND DOLLARS FOR A KISS, AND FIFTY CENTS FOR YOUR SOUL.

I KNOW, BECAUSE I TURNED DOWN THE FIRST OFFER OFTEN ENOUGH AND HELD OUT FOR THE FIFTY CENTS."

—Marilyn Monroe, *My Story*, 1974, released posthumously, co-written by Ben Hecht

# NO DUMB BLONDE!

Defying the stereotype, Marilyn was smart: she read widely and made friends with intellectuals, even marrying one in Arthur Miller. An auction of her personal effects in 1999 included a lot of 430 books, in which there were several first editions and copies annotated by her own hand. The collection reveals her inner bookworm as well as a broad range of interests and concerns. So what was on her shelves?

**430 BOOKS IN HER LIBRARY**

A STREETCAR NAMED DESIRE
TENNESSEE WILLIAMS

HOW STANISLAVSKY DIRECTS
MIKHAIL GORCHAKOV

THE SUN ALSO RISES
ERNEST HEMINGWAY

FYODOR DOSTOEVSKY

THE PORTABLE
WALT WHITMAN

RELAX AND LIVE
JOSEPH A. KENNEDY

ULYSSES
JAMES JOYCE

THE LETTERS OF SIGMUND FREUD

WHY I AM NOT A CHRISTIAN
BERTRAND RUSSELL

THE STORY OF A NOVEL
THOMAS WOLFE

DAS KAPITAL
KARL MARX

BABY & CHILD CARE
DR BENJAMIN SPOCK

TROUBLED WOMEN
LUCY FREEMAN

THE ART OF LOVING
ERICH FROMM

THE CAPTIVE
MARCEL PROUST

METAPHYSICS
ARISTOTLE

THE SHORT NOVELS OF COLETTE

THE PROPHET
KAHLIL GIBRAN

OUT OF MY LATER YEARS
ALBERT EINSTEIN

PORTRAIT OF THE ARTIST AS A YOUNG DOG
DYLAN THOMAS

When she died, Marilyn was reading *To Kill a Mockingbird* by Harper Lee and *Captain Newman MD* by Leo Rosten (the main character was based on her psychiatrist, Ralph Greenson).

TO KILL A MOCKINGBIRD
HARPER LEE

# MILITARY MONROE

Marilyn's ties to the military weave throughout her early life and career, from her young first marriage to the peak of her popularity with American troops abroad.

## 1942

To escape the cycle of foster care, at the age of 16, Marilyn wed James Dougherty. A year later, Jim joined the US Merchant Marine and the young newlyweds lived on Catalina Island off Los Angeles, prior to him serving overseas during the Second World War.

## FIRST PHOTOSHOOT

In 1944, Marilyn was working at the Radioplane munitions factory when she was discovered by army photographer David Conover. Conover had been sent by Captain Ronald Reagan to capture morale-boosting images of women contributing to the war effort.

## ENTERTAINER

In 1952, Marilyn appeared at Camp Pendleton, a Marine base south of Los Angeles. She entertained thousands of soldiers with her sensual performance of 'Do It Again' by George Gershwin and Buddy DeSylva.

## PIN-UP STAR

Marilyn became the American GI's number one pin-up star during the Korean War (1950–53). She featured in a host of military magazines, winning several awards for her 'cheesecake' (slang for pin-up) credentials.

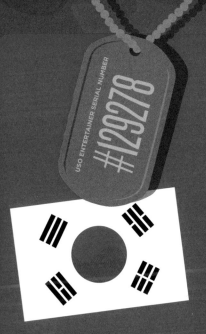

USO ENTERTAINER SERIAL NUMBER

#129278

# PERFORMING IN KOREA

During her Japanese honeymoon with Joe DiMaggio, Marilyn was invited to perform for the troops stationed in Korea. In February 1954 she embarked on a tour of the peninsula, finding freedom in leaving the world of Hollywood – and her new husband – behind.

# 4
DAYS

# 10
SHOWS

# 100,000
SERVICEMEN

## "STANDING IN THE SNOWFALL FACING THESE YELLING SOLDIERS, I FELT FOR THE FIRST TIME IN MY LIFE NO FEAR OF ANYTHING. I FELT ONLY HAPPY."

—Marilyn Monroe talking about her experience in Korea

WORLD

# MARILYN'S FAVOURITE THINGS

## FOOD

**Caviar and hotdogs!**

## DRINK

**Dom Perignon 1953**

## SHOP

**Bloomingdale's, New York**

## PERFUME

**Chanel No. 5**

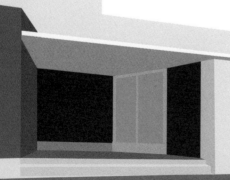

## RESTAURANT

**Romanoff's, Hollywood**

# COLOURS

## ACTORS/ACTRESSES

Clark Gable, Charlie Chaplin, Marlon Brando, Cary Grant.

Greta Garbo, Jean Harlow, Marie Dressler, Ginger Rogers

## SINGERS

Frank Sinatra,
Ella Fitzgerald
(pictured)

## MUSICIANS

Louis Armstrong,
Earl Bostic,
Beethoven,
Mozart (pictured)

## ARTISTS

Botticelli,
El Greco, Goya,
Michelangelo,
Picasso
(pictured)

# BEAUTY SECRETS

Marilyn was a perfectionist when it came to her appearance, and this could at times tip over into intense anxiety. A full transformation by her make-up artist Allan Snyder, who worked with Marilyn throughout her career, could take up to three hours to achieve. How was her signature look created?

**HAIR**

A natural brunette, Marilyn went blonde in 1948 and never looked back – her short, platinum curls became the iconic style of the 1950s. Her hair would be bleached up to once a week, with a whitening powder used for touch-ups when needed. She underwent electrolysis to raise her hairline and temper her widow's peak but left the downy facial fuzz on her cheeks – reportedly a consequence of using a hormone cream – as she liked the way it caught the light to give her an on–camera glow.

**BROW**

Her eyebrows were shaped into subtle peaks, which Marilyn believed helped to minimize the width of her forehead.

**EYES**

A white shadow was used across her lids up to the brow bone, with a taupe shade to define the sockets. Winged flicks of eyeliner were applied on and beyond the upper lash line, mirrored with a lighter brown liner extending from the bottom corner, giving the illusion of a shadow. White eyeliner highlighted the inner corners. She would apply false eyelashes to the outer edges of her eyes only, after mascara.

**SKIN**

To cleanse, Marilyn used soap with up to 30 splashes of water. Witch hazel was used as a toner and to keep blemishes at bay. Having normal-to-dry skin, she followed up with a heavy moisturiser, which she also used as a primer, highlighter, and to add a sheen to eyelids. Marilyn religiously avoided overexposure to the sun before it was widely considered damaging, in order to feel "blonde all over".

**FACE**

After applying foundation, Marilyn's cheeks would be contoured with blusher and highlighter, and her forehead received the same treatment. A touch of colour was added to the tip of her nose to make it look shorter.

**SPOT**

Whether real or not, Marilyn's beauty spot was likely enhanced by make-up. It became a trademark of her look and has been widely copied.

**LIPS**

Marilyn's signature pout was achieved using up to five shades of red to achieve the illusion of fuller lips. She contoured them with a brush, using darker shades on the outer edges, graduating to a lighter hue in the middle. Her favourite lipstick was said to be Guerlain's 'Diabolique'.

# MARILYN IN L.A.

## HOTEL BEL-AIR
*701 Stone Canyon Rd, Bel Air*

Marilyn called the Hotel Bel-Air her home in 1952 and would continue to stay there over the following decade. The hotel was the site for 'The Last Sitting' – her famous final photoshoot with Bert Stern, commissioned by *Vogue* magazine in June 1962.

## BEVERLY CARLTON HOTEL
*9400 Olympic Blvd, Beverly Hills*

This hotel was home to Marilyn three times between 1949 and 1952.

## WESTWOOD MEMORIAL PARK
*1218 Glendon Ave, Westwood*

Marilyn's bronze casket was interred here in crypt number 24 at the Corridor of Memories on 8 August 1962.

## BEVERLY HILLS HOTEL
*9641 West Sunset Blvd, Beverly Hills*

Marilyn lived at this world-famous hotel – a favourite of both royals and Hollywood royalty – between 1952 and 1954. She would continue to stay throughout her career, no. 7 being her favourite bungalow.

## MARILYN'S FINAL RESIDENCE
*12305 5th Helena Drive, Brentwood*

Her Brentwood home was the place she died and the only house she ever owned.

## GRAUMAN'S CHINESE THEATRE
*6925 Hollywood Blvd, Hollywood*

Having visited this illustrious cinema during childhood, Marilyn would be immortalized on the pavement outside in 1953, leaving her handprints in the cement with *Gentlemen Prefer Blondes* co-star Jane Russell.

## FORMOSA CAFÉ
*7156 Santa Monica Blvd, West Hollywood*

This legendary eatery was a regular haunt for Marilyn in 1958 while filming *Some Like It Hot.*

## BARNEY'S BEANERY
*8447 Santa Monica Blvd, West Hollywood*

Hollywood institution Barney's has fed stars through the generations including Marilyn's idol Jean Harlow. The chilli was a favourite meal when Marilyn was a starlet.

## CHASEN'S
*9039 Beverly Blvd, West Hollywood*

The preferred venue of the 'in' crowd. Marilyn celebrated her success following *Gentlemen Prefer Blondes* and went on her first date with Joe DiMaggio here.

## ROMANOFF'S
*326 North Rodeo Drive, Beverly Hills*

An exclusive restaurant run by self-styled prince Mike Romanoff and his wife Gloria. Marilyn first frequented it with agent Johnny Hyde. In 1954 it was the venue for a huge party thrown in her honour, where she met and danced with her idol Clark Gable.

## TWENTIETH CENTURY FOX STUDIOS
*10201 W Pico Blvd*

Hotel ●    Food ●    Studio ●    Cinema ●    Home ●    Grave ●

# ICONIC LOOKS

DESIGNED BY
- William Travilla
- Orry-Kelly

## NIAGARA

**(AS ROSE LOOMIS)**

This magenta wiggle dress with cut-out detailing causes the character Ray to ask his wife, "Why don't you ever wear a dress like that?" "Listen, for a dress like that, you've got to start laying plans when you're about 13," she replies.

## GENTLEMEN PREFER BLONDES

**(AS LORELEI LEE)**

Worn during her performance of 'Diamonds Are a Girl's Best Friend', this sleeveless floor-length pink gown, accessorized with long matching gloves and gleaming rocks, has inspired many homages – famously by Madonna in the 'Material Girl' music video.

## HOW TO MARRY A MILLIONAIRE

**(AS POLA DEBEVOISE)**

Marilyn sports this red swimsuit with diamanté trim in a fashion-show scene and images of her wearing it were widely used in the film's promotion. In this outfit she is the epitome of 1950s pin-up glamour.

Marilyn's style both on and off set made her an enduring fashion icon. Her outfits were widely publicized and emulated in her time, as they still are today. Eschewing underwear, her tailoring was often tight and necklines plunging – enhancing her hourglass figure and pushing the boundaries of what was acceptable for a woman to wear. When not in front of the camera, Marilyn favoured something a little simpler, such as slacks and a sweater or – her loungewear of choice – a white cotton bath robe. Famously, she slept in the nude. Here's a small selection of her legendary film looks. All apart from one were created by Hollywood costume designer William Travilla.

## THE SEVEN YEAR ITCH

**(AS THE GIRL)**

The most famous of Marilyn's film costumes, and perhaps the most well-known dress in cinema history, was worn during the legendary subway scene. In the film itself only her legs are shown, leaving everything else to the imagination.

## BUS STOP

**(AS CHERIE)**

Marilyn was no stranger to show-stopping showgirl outfits, having worn them in several films prior to *Bus Stop*. This green, black and gold sequinned leotard with removable tailpiece was worn with fishnet stockings during her rendition of 'Old Black Magic'.

## SOME LIKE IT HOT

**(AS SUGAR KANE)**

The fringing on this black dress with a deep V neckline is reminiscent of the 1920s, the era in which Marilyn's highest grossing film is set. Costume designer Orry-Kelly won an Oscar for his vintage-inspired creations.

1955

1956

1959

# JOE DIMAGGIO

Married at 16, Marilyn divorced her first husband aged 20 to pursue her career. After she became famous both of her subsequent marriages also ended in divorce, despite her yearning for a stable relationship. Baseball star Joe DiMaggio disapproved of her sex symbol image, leading to jealous outbursts and resulting in a tumultuously short union.

**AGE**
**84**

**PROFESSION:**
Baseball centre fielder, New York Yankees

**YEARS WORKED:**
1936–51

**9** World Series championships 1936–39, 1941, 1947, 1949–51

Major League Baseball Most Valuable Player Award: 1939, 1941, 1947

**DIED: 8 MARCH 1999**

## MARRIED MARILYN 14 JANUARY 1954

**GROUNDS FOR DIVORCE:**
Mental cruelty

**MARRIAGE LASTED**
**9**
**MONTHS**

Joe's devotion to Marilyn continued after their split and also after her death – he sent roses to her grave three times a week for 20 years.

"Our marriage was a sort of crazy, difficult friendship with sexual privileges. Later I learned that's what marriages often are."

—Marilyn Monroe

**YEARS OLDER**
**11**

**BORN: 25 NOVEMBER 1914**

MARILYN

50

# ARTHUR MILLER

Her marriage to playwright Arthur Miller lasted much longer but was plagued by insecurities, fuelled by her drug dependency and inability to have children. How do these titans in their fields and their marriages to Marilyn measure up?

**DIED: 10 FEBRUARY 2005**

**AGE**
## 89

**Pulitzer Prize for Drama – *Death of a Salesman*, 1949**

**American Theater Hall of Fame, inducted 1979**

**PROFESSION:** Playwright, screenwriter, author and essayist

**YEARS WORKED:** 1938–2004

**Kennedy Center Honors**

**National Medal of the Arts**
**1993**

1 9 8 4

## MARRIED MARILYN
## 29 JUNE 1956

**GROUNDS FOR DIVORCE:** Incompatibility

**BORN: 17 OCTOBER 1915**

**MARRIAGE LASTED**
## 4½
**YEARS**

Marilyn and Arthur got married twice – they had both a civil ceremony and a traditional Jewish wedding, for which she converted to Judaism.

**YEARS OLDER**
## 10

"He's a brilliant man and a wonderful writer, but I think he is a better writer than a husband."

—Marilyn Monroe

# MARILYN IN THE UK

In July 1956, two weeks after Marilyn married Arthur Miller, the newlyweds flew to England – she to film *The Prince and the Showgirl* with Sir Laurence Olivier, and her husband to promote his controversial play *A View from the Bridge*. The visit attracted much press attention and crowds of adoring fans. However, it was marred by private and professional stress as cracks began to appear in their fledgling marriage, and on-set tensions between Marilyn and Olivier boiled over.

## ✈ LONDON AIRPORT
### (NOW HEATHROW)

| | |
|---|---|
| ARRIVAL DATE: | 14 JULY 1956 |
| ARRIVAL TIME: | 10.40 |
| LUGGAGE: | 27 pieces, costing $1,500 in excess baggage fees |
| WELCOME PARTY: | Laurence Olivier and his wife Vivien Leigh |
| | 150 reporters |
| | 70 policemen |
| | 3,000 fans |

Marilyn met Queen Elizabeth II at the Empire cinema in Leicester Square, London, on 29 October after the premiere of *The Battle of the River Plate.* The two of them, both 30 at the time, talked cordially about the fact that they were currently neighbours.

Parkside House, Wick Lane, Englefield Green, Egham, would be the couple's home for 4 months.

Marilyn had a strained working relationship with Laurence Olivier that lasted throughout filming at Pinewood Studios. Her time-keeping and constant deferment to acting coach Paula Strasberg jarred with his classically trained background, and she thought he could be cruel.

Marilyn became ill on 25 August, which led to a break in filming. A rumoured miscarriage was never confirmed. It was more likely to have been a combination of depression, exhaustion and substance misuse, and perhaps a flare up of her chronic endometriosis.

## "IT SEEMED TO BE RAINING THE WHOLE TIME. OR MAYBE IT WAS ME."

**—Marilyn Monroe**

A sour note was struck in the Millers' marriage when Marilyn discovered a journal in which her husband was critical of his new wife. It sent her into a spiral of insecurity, not helped when he flew back to America for 10 days to see his children from a previous marriage, the day after she became ill.

## PLACES VISITED BY MARILYN

PINEWOOD STUDIOS

NATIONAL GALLERY

WINDSOR GREAT PARK

SALISBURY CATHEDRAL

BRIGHTON SEAFRONT

FOYLES BOOKSHOP

SHELLEY'S HOTEL, LEWES

DEPARTURE:

20 NOVEMBER 1956,

Pan American flight

from London Airport

# MEDICATING MARILYN

Drugs were endemic in Hollywood from its inception, with pills prescribed to keep stars working and wind them down after long days on set. Suffering crippling anxiety and insomnia, Marilyn was given sedatives to calm her nerves, escape her depression and help her sleep. Barbiturates would take hold of her life, disrupting her work and ultimately killing her. Marilyn reportedly first took pills in her late teens. She was certainly addicted by 1954, and in the last years of her life her usage had spiralled to tragic proportions. These are some of the drugs that she took.

## Nembutal
### (Barbiturate)

In her final years Marilyn's dosage was upped to 300mg, 3 times the normal strength. Two days before she died, Marilyn picked up two prescriptions from different doctors. Her autopsy showed 4.5mg in her blood – 10 times the recommended dosage – with 13mg in her liver, a cumulative result of extended use.

## Amytal
### (Barbiturate)

After suffering her second miscarriage, Marilyn feared it was her use of this drug that caused it. While filming *The Misfits*, she began injecting Amytal at levels comparable to those of a general anaesthetic.

## Chloral hydrate
### (Geminal diol)

Marilyn's psychiatrist, Ralph Greenson, began prescribing chloral hydrate to try to reduce her barbiturate intake. The attempt failed. Marilyn's autopsy showed 8mg in her blood – 20 times the recommended dosage.

## YOUTH SHOTS

During the last month of her life, Marilyn's doctor Hyman Engelberg administered daily 'youth shots' to alter her darkened mood and give her energy. These injections were likely to have contained amphetamines.

## Phenobarbital

### (Barbiturate)

## Librium

### (Barbiturate)

## Phenergan

### (Antihistamine)

## Dexamyl

### (Amphetamine/ Barbiturate)

**Ralph Greenson also prescribed Marilyn this potent mix of the barbiturate Amobarbital and the stimulant Dextroamphetamine.**

## Valium

### (Benzodiazepine)

**Marilyn reportedly took this drug while working on the set of her unfinished film *Something's Got to Give*, washed down with the ubiquitous champagne.**

# CHAMPAGNE

**Taking pills combined with alcohol increases their potency – champagne was Marilyn's drink of choice, though she also consumed sherry, vodka and vermouth.**

**Other Hollywood icons who died from a barbiturate overdose include Judy Garland and Montgomery Clift, Marilyn's co-star in *The Misfits*.**

# LATE AGAIN

From her earliest days as a model, Marilyn was notorious for being late – a trait that became a legendary part of her personality and a source of friction in her professional career. Some saw it as rude. Others who knew her better understood that it was often down to crippling performance anxiety and a string of health issues. Her time-keeping became worse the more she came to rely on alcohol and prescription drugs to cope with her increasing level of fame.

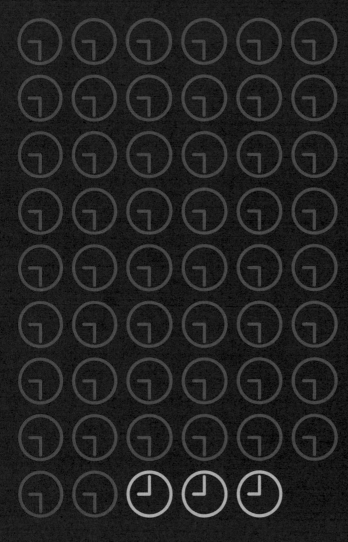

Late

On time

While filming *The Prince and the Showgirl*, Marilyn was on time for only 3 out of the 53 days on set.

"LOOK, IF WE WANTED SOMEBODY TO BE ON TIME AND TO KNOW THE LINES JUST PERFECTLY, I'VE GOT AN OLD AUNT IN VIENNA. SHE'S GOING TO BE THERE AT FIVE IN THE MORNING AND NEVER MISS A WORD. BUT WHO WANTS TO LOOK AT HER?"

—Billy Wilder, director

"SHE WAS ALWAYS LATE, BUT I THINK IT WAS IN TERROR. SHE COULDN'T FACE DOING WHAT SHE WAS CALLED UPON TO DO; SHE COULDN'T COPE."

—Lauren Bacall, actress and co-star

# MARILYN
# MONROE

---

# 03
# WORK

# "PLEASE DON'T MAKE ME A JOKE... I DON'T MIND MAKING JOKES, BUT I DON'T WANT TO LOOK LIKE ONE... I WANT TO BE AN ARTIST, AN ACTRESS WITH INTEGRITY... IF FAME GOES BY, SO LONG, I'VE HAD YOU, FAME. IF IT GOES BY, I'VE ALWAYS KNOWN IT WAS FICKLE."

—Marilyn Monroe, final interview with Richard Meryman, *LIFE* magazine, 1962

# COVER STAR

Marilyn signed up to the Blue Book Modeling Agency in August 1945, after being discovered whilst working in the Radioplane munitions factory. First marketed as 'the girl next door' type, the agency soon realized her pin-up potential. Within six months she had appeared on 33 magazine covers for publications including *U.S. Camera, Laff, Pageant* and *Peek.*

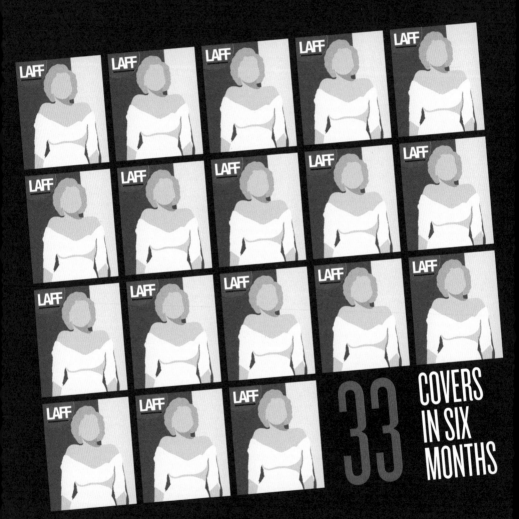

# 33 COVERS IN SIX MONTHS

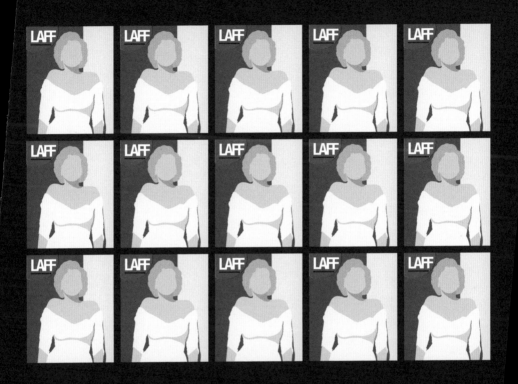

Marilyn was the first cover star of *Playboy* magazine in December 1953. The issue contained nude photos, taken for a calendar in 1949 when she was a struggling starlet.

# FILMOGRAPHY

Marilyn's big break came in 1950 when she had a small but important part in *The Asphalt Jungle*, a film noir directed by John Huston.

## 1947
*Dangerous Years*

## 1948
*Scudda Hoo!*
*Scudda Hay!*

## 1948
*Ladies of the Chorus*

## 1950
*The Asphalt Jungle*

## 1950
*A Ticket to Tomahawk*

## 1949
*Love Happy*

## 1950
*All About Eve*

## 1950
*The Fireball*

## 1951
*Right Cross*

## 1951
*Love Nest*

## 1951
*As Young as You Feel*

## 1951
*Home Town Story*

## 1951
*Let's Make It Legal*

## 1952
*Clash by Night*

## 1952
*We're Not Married!*

**1952**
*Don't Bother to Knock*

**1952**
*Monkey Business*

**1952**
*O. Henry's Full House*

**1953**
*How to Marry a Millionaire*

**1953**
*Gentlemen Prefer Blondes*

**1953**
*Niagara*

**1954**
*River of No Return*

**1954**
*There's No Business Like Show Business*

**1955**
*The Seven Year Itch*

**1959**
*Some Like It Hot*

**1957**
*The Prince and the Showgirl*

**1956**
*Bus Stop*

**1960**
*Let's Make Love*

**1961**
*The Misfits*

**1962**
*Something's Got to Give*

UNFINISHED

Her first starring role was in 1952's *Don't Bother to Knock* and the release of three successful pictures the following year confirmed her star status. In total she made 29 films – her 30th was unfinished.

WORK

JANE RUSSELL        MARILYN MONROE

# GENTLEMEN PREFER BLONDES

DIRECTED BY
HOWARD HAWKS

RELEASED
1953

Marilyn plays gold-digging entertainer Lorelei Lee in this engaging musical comedy, originally intended as a vehicle for Betty Grable. Jane Russell co-stars as her witty, down-to-earth friend Dorothy, contrasting with Marilyn's 'dumb blonde' persona. Lorelei is a role, however, that she made entirely her own, winning the hearts of audiences and critics on release. The story follows the pair's ocean voyage to Paris, and features lavish musical numbers, plenty of plot twists... and diamonds!

# MAIN CAST:

**MARILYN MONROE**
as Lorelei Lee

**JANE RUSSELL**
as Dorothy Shaw

The song 'Bye, Bye Baby' was recorded by several singers in the 1950s, including Marilyn's friend Frank Sinatra, spending more than six weeks in the charts.

**$2.3m**

**$5.3m**

BUDGET      BOX OFFICE

# 740

The number of performances in the run of the Broadway musical *Gentlemen Prefer Blondes*. It opened at the Ziegfeld Theater on 8 December 1949 and starred Carol Channing.

Marilyn's iconic song and dance number 'Diamonds Are a Girl's Best Friend' almost didn't feature her voice at all. Fox wanted it entirely dubbed but 'ghost singer' Marni Nixon objected, in the end only dubbing two of the more operatic phrases.

The story had started life as a 1925 serialization in *Harper's Bazaar* by Anita Loos and was also made into a 1928 silent film, now thought lost.

The ocean liner is based on the SS *Ile de France* and the ship model was previously featured in the film *Titanic* (1953), starring Barbara Stanwyck.

# SALARIES

Marilyn's contracts consisted of a weekly base payment, which could be negotiated up to a contractual ceiling for each film. This financial structure was the very foundation of the Hollywood studio system, which saw actors as property rather than talent. Leading males would receive much higher salaries but even compared to some of her female peers, Marilyn was poorly paid.

*Gentlemen Prefer Blondes*
**Total payment**

MARILYN MONROE
# $18,000

JANE RUSSELL
# $200,000

PAYMENT PER WEEK

| 1946 | 1947 | 1948 | 1950 | 1951 |
|---|---|---|---|---|
| Twentieth Century Fox, first contract | Twentieth Century Fox, contract renewal | Columbia contract | MGM, *The Asphalt Jungle* | Twentieth Century Fox, second contract |
| **$75** | **$150** | **$125** | **$350** | **$500** |

## 1956

Twentieth Century Fox, third contract

- Non-exclusive
- 4 films over 10 years
- $100,000 per film base rate
- $500 a week for expenses
- Approval over all major aspects of production

MARILYN

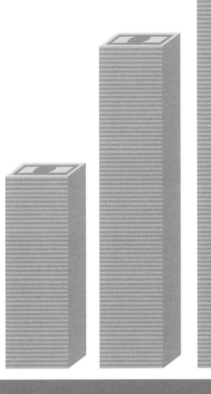

# MARILYN MONROE PRODUCTIONS

In January 1955, Marilyn held a press conference to announce her new company Marilyn Monroe Productions. Jointly owned with friend and photographer Milton Greene, the aim was to gain greater financial and creative control. Twentieth Century Fox was outraged but eventually conceded to a new non-exclusive contract (allowing her to pursue independent projects) of single payments with a profit share. Marilyn had taken on the studio system and won.

**OWNERSHIP:**

| MARILYN MONROE | MILTON GREENE |
|---|---|
| 51% | 49% |

The results of Marilyn's new contract, negotiated through her own company, can be seen in her higher wages.

| 1952 | 1953 | 1953 |
|---|---|---|
| Twentieth Century Fox, *We're Not Married* | Twentieth Century Fox, *Gentlemen Prefer Blondes* | Twentieth Century Fox, updated contract |
| **$750** | **$1,250** | **$1,500** |

| 959 | *Some Like it Hot* | **$100,000** | flat fee plus 10% profits |
|---|---|---|---|
| 961 | *The Misfits* | **$300,000** | flat fee plus 10% profits |
| 962 | *Something's Got to Give* | **$500,000** | (unfinished) |

# GENRES

An outcome of the Hollywood studio system was that actors could easily become typecast, and Marilyn would battle for more serious roles the higher her star rose. In 1954 she refused to make the film *The Girl in Pink Tights* – another musical comedy in which she was to play a sexy 'dumb blonde'. Fed up of being defined by a specific genre and character type, she started her own production company. How does her output divide up in terms of genre?

**32%**
**COMEDY**

**20%**
**DRAMA**

**14%**
**ROMANCE**

## "IT'S NOT THAT I OBJECT TO DOING MUSICALS AND COMEDIES – IN FACT, I RATHER ENJOY THEM – BUT I'D LIKE TO DO DRAMATIC PARTS TOO."

—Marilyn Monroe, live TV appearance on *Person to Person* with Edward R. Murrow, discussing her new company, 1955

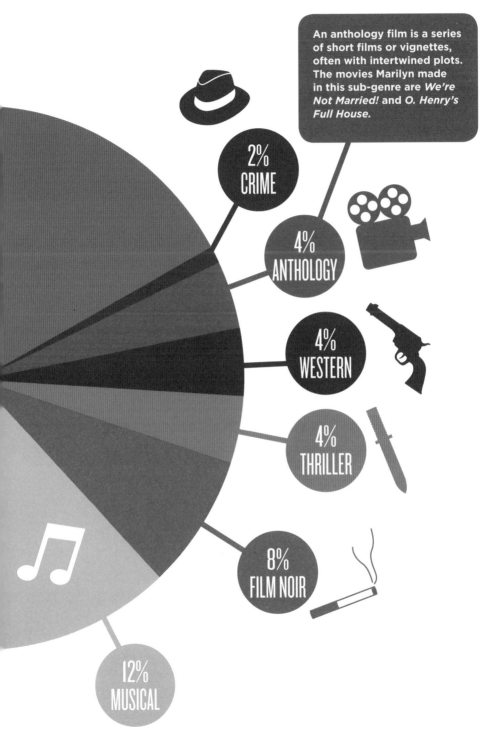

An anthology film is a series of short films or vignettes, often with intertwined plots. The movies Marilyn made in this sub-genre are *We're Not Married!* and *O. Henry's Full House.*

2%
CRIME

4%
ANTHOLOGY

4%
WESTERN

4%
THRILLER

8%
FILM NOIR

12%
MUSICAL

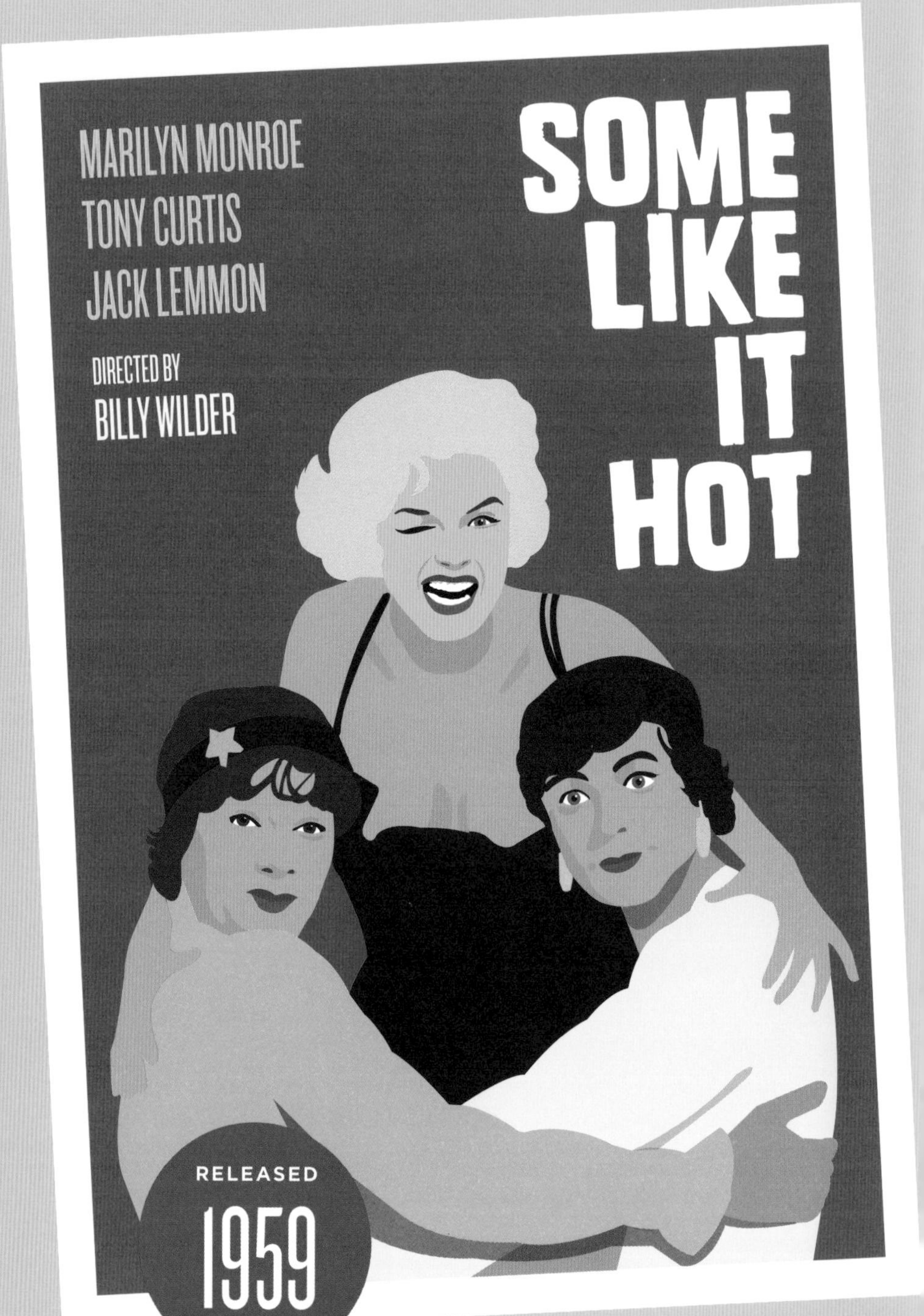

MARILYN MONROE
TONY CURTIS
JACK LEMMON

DIRECTED BY
BILLY WILDER

SOME LIKE IT HOT

RELEASED
1959

This brilliantly funny black-and-white romantic comedy – set in prohibition-era Chicago – silenced Marilyn's critics and was the third-highest grossing film of 1959. Co-stars Jack Lemmon and Tony Curtis assume the disguise of female musicians, taking refuge in Marilyn's character Sugar Kane's band in order to escape the mob. Although at this point her on-set behaviour was becoming increasingly erratic, she delivers a performance of comedic genius, and it was her biggest box office success.

## MAIN CAST:

**MARILYN MONROE**
as Sugar 'Kane' Kowalczyk, singer and ukulele player

**TONY CURTIS**
as Joe/Josephine/Shell Oil Junior, saxophone player

**JACK LEMMON**
as Jerry/Daphne, double bass player

## No. 1

A 2017 BBC poll of 253 film critics from 52 countries voted the film the Number 1 comedy of all time.

The Jazz Age soundtrack was created by veteran Broadway and Hollywood composer, conductor and arranger Adolph Deutsch. Marilyn performs four songs.

## $2.9m $40m

BUDGET BOX OFFICE

Two of the gangsters are played by actors who previously starred in seminal crime films: George Raft (*Scarface*, 1932) and George E. Stone (*Little Caesar*, 1931).

## 47

The number of takes apparently needed for Marilyn to deliver the line "It's me, Sugar."

## "NOBODY'S PERFECT."

The famous final line was only meant as a placeholder until a better idea came along... it never did.

Mitzi Gaynor was Billy Wilder's first choice for Sugar Kane, and both Frank Sinatra and Danny Kaye were considered for Jack Lemmon's role.

# DIRECTING MARILYN

Marilyn's behaviour on and off set could make her difficult to direct. She intensely disliked being patronized and from 1956, after the formation of her production company and subsequent new contract with Fox, Marilyn would be given final approval on the choice of director for all her films. Her directors' recollections offer an insight into Marilyn the actor, and their working relationship with her.

"ALL I CAN TELL YOU IS IF MARILYN WAS AROUND TODAY, I'D BE ON MY KNEES, SAYING 'PLEASE LET'S DO IT AGAIN!'"

"SHE HAD NO TALENT AS AN ACTRESS, BUT SHE HAD ONE THING THAT THE CAMERA GETS. SHE WAS A BORN STAR."

### BILLY WILDER

• *The Seven Year Itch*, 1955
• *Some Like It Hot*, 1959

### OTTO PREMINGER

• *River of No Return*, 1954

"MONROE'S PROBLEM WAS THAT MANY DIRECTORS HANDLED HER AS IF SHE WAS REAL. SHE WASN'T. SHE WAS ONLY COMFORTABLE IN UNREAL ROLES."

"SHE WENT RIGHT DOWN INTO HER PERSONAL EXPERIENCE FOR EVERYTHING, REACHED DOWN AND PULLED SOMETHING OUT OF HERSELF THAT WAS UNIQUE AND EXTRAORDINARY... IT WAS ALL THE TRUTH."

### HOWARD HAWKS

• *Monkey Business*, 1952
• *Gentlemen Prefer Blondes*, 1953

### JOHN HUSTON

• *The Asphalt Jungle*, 1950
• *The Misfits*, 1961

# "DID YOU EVER SEE ON THE SCREEN 'THIS PICTURE WAS DIRECTED BY AN IGNORANT DIRECTOR WITH NO TASTE'? NO, THE PUBLIC ALWAYS BLAMES THE STAR."

—Marilyn Monroe

"YOU KNOW, I ACTUALLY FANCIED HER WHEN I FIRST MET HER. SHE'S A FREAK OF NATURE, NOT A GENIUS. A BEAUTIFUL FREAK."

## LAURENCE OLIVIER
- *The Prince and the Showgirl*, 1957

"SHE HAD AN ABSOLUTE UNERRING TOUCH WITH COMEDY... SHE ACTED AS IF SHE DIDN'T QUITE UNDERSTAND WHY IT WAS FUNNY, WHICH IS WHAT MADE IT SO FUNNY."

## GEORGE CUKOR
- *Let's Make Love*, 1960
- *Something's Got to Give*, 1962 (unfinished)

"MARILYN WAS THE MOST FRIGHTENED LITTLE GIRL. AND YET SCARED AS SHE WAS, SHE HAD THIS STRANGE EFFECT WHEN SHE WAS PHOTOGRAPHED... IN FACT, THE CAMERA LOVED HER."

## JOSEPH L. MANKIEWICZ
- *All About Eve*, 1950

"SHE WAS A VERY PECULIAR MIX OF SHYNESS AND — I WOULDN'T SAY 'STAR ALLURE' — BUT SHE KNEW, EXACTLY, HER IMPACT ON MEN."

## FRITZ LANG
- *Clash by Night*, 1952

# HAPPY BIRTHDAY MR PRESIDENT

Though she was not given much credit for her vocal talent during her lifetime, Marilyn took singing seriously and performed a surprising quantity of musical numbers on screen with great flair. Her biggest musical influences were good friends Frank Sinatra and Ella Fitzgerald – she helped Ella gain access to clubs when racial segregation was still in force.

Perhaps Marilyn's most famous musical moment was singing her breathy rendition of 'Happy Birthday Mr President' to John F. Kennedy at Madison Square Garden in May 1962. "I can now retire from politics after having had 'Happy Birthday' sung to me in such a sweet, wholesome way," JFK announced to the crowd.

"I WON'T BE SATISFIED UNTIL PEOPLE WANT TO HEAR ME SING WITHOUT LOOKING AT ME. OF COURSE, THAT DOESN'T MEAN I WANT THEM TO STOP LOOKING."

—Marilyn Monroe, 1954

**MOVIES & SONGS**

### 1948 — Ladies of the Chorus

'Anyone Can See I Love You'

'Every Baby Needs a Da-Da-Daddy'

### 1950 — A Ticket to Tomahawk

'Oh What a Forward Man You Are'

### 1953 — Niagara

'Kiss'

### 1953 — Gentlemen Prefer Blondes

'We're Just Two Little Girls from Little Rock'

'When Love Goes Wrong'

'Bye, Bye Baby'

'Diamonds Are a Girl's Best Friend'

### 1954 — River of No Return

'River of No Return'

'I'm Going to File My Claim'

'One Silver Dollar'

'Down in the Meadow'

### 1954 — There's No Business Like Show Business

'After You Get What You Want You Don't Want It'

'Heatwave'

'Lazy'

'There's No Business Like Show Business'

'A Man Chases a Girl'

'You'd be Surprised'

### 1956 — Bus Stop

'That Old Black Magic'

### 1957 — The Prince and the Showgirl

'I Found a Dream'

### 1960 — Let's Make Love

'Let's Make Love'

'Incurably Romantic'

'Specialization'

'My Heart Belongs to Daddy'

### 1959 — Some Like It Hot

'I'm Through With Love'

'I Want to be Loved by You'

'Running Wild'

CLARK GABLE    MARILYN MONROE    MONTGOMERY CLIFT

# The Misfits

DIRECTED BY JOHN HUSTON

RELEASED
1961

Tragedy and brilliance run through this drama, in which Marilyn (as Roslyn) finds herself in Reno, Nevada, finalizing her divorce. She bands together with a group of characters including an ageing cowboy (Clark Gable), all escaping to the desert. Visually stunning and emotionally poignant, it was the most expensive black and white film ever made, and a complete box office disaster. Written by husband Arthur Miller, *The Misfits* marked the end of their marriage and was both Monroe and Gable's final completed film.

# MAIN CAST:

**MARILYN MONROE**
as Roslyn Taber

**CLARK GABLE**
as Gay Langland

**MONTGOMERY CLIFT**
as Perce Howland

The prestigious Magnum photographic agency sent nine of its most talented photographers to cover life both on and off the set. Eve Arnold, Henri Cartier-Bresson, Elliot Erwitt, Ernst Haas, Cornell Capa, Bruce Davidson, Erich Hartmann, Dennis Stock and Inge Morath (who would become Miller's third wife) were given exclusive access to the production.

# $4m
## BUDGET

# $4.1m
## BOX OFFICE

Mid-July temperatures on location in the Nevada desert soared to 108°F (42°C). Filming had been pushed back to the height of summer due to delays on Marilyn's previous film *Let's Make Love* (1960), caused by a Screen Actors Guild strike.

108°F / 42°C

Clark Gable suffered a heart attack two days after filming finished, dying ten days later on 16 November 1960. *The Misfits* was released on 1 February 1961, on what would have been his 60th birthday. As with agent and mentor Johnny Hyde, Marilyn felt a sense of guilt over the passing of her childhood idol.

Due to both Marilyn and Montgomery Clift's drug and alcohol addictions, a doctor was on call 24 hours a day. In August 1960, production shut down for two weeks when Marilyn was sent to hospital to detox and recover from a breakdown.

# THE ACTORS STUDIO

After walking out on her studio, feeling alienated from her sex symbol image, Marilyn escaped to New York in 1955. There she announced her new production company, underwent psychoanalysis and studied to become a serious actor at the prestigious Actors Studio on West 44th Street. Director Lee Strasberg taught 'The Method' – a way of acting that encourages pupils to draw on their personal emotional experiences to help them perform without inhibition – using techniques developed out of the practices of Russian actor and director Konstantin Stanislavski. Lee's wife Paula would become Marilyn's acting coach on the set of all her subsequent films, often to the annoyance of her directors. Who are some of the other alumni?

# THE ACTORS STUDIO
### STARRING
## MARILYN MONROE
## JAMES DEAN • JACK NICHOLSON
## DUSTIN HOFFMAN • JANE FONDA
## MONTGOMERY CLIFT • AL PACINO
## STEVE MCQUEEN
## PAUL NEWMAN
## ANNE BANCROFT
## MARLON BRANDO
### AND
## GEORGE
## PEPPARD
(pictured)

# MARILYN MONROE

## 04
# LEGACY

"IT WAS A SURPRISE WHEN SHE PASSED AWAY, SINCE SHE WAS SO YOUNG. THAT MADE IT EVEN MORE TRAGIC FOR US, AND WE WERE GREATLY SADDENED.

# MAR

# I OFTEN WONDER WHAT MS MONROE WOULD HAVE BEEN LIKE IF SHE WAS ALIVE TODAY ... CLEARLY SHE WOULD BE THE QUEEN OF HOLLYWOOD."

—Joe Coudert, photographer, quoted in *Marilyn Monroe: Private and Undisclosed* by Michelle Morgan, 2007

# RECORD BREAKERS

Marilyn Monroe's enduring appeal is always in evidence when her memorabilia goes under the hammer. The allure of her wardrobe, in particular, excites buyers into a bidding frenzy: she wore around half of the 25 most expensive dresses ever auctioned, two of which hold world records.

## HAPPY BIRTHDAY MR PRESIDENT

**WORN:** 1962

**SOLD:** 2016

MOST EXPENSIVE DRESS (AND ITEM OF CLOTHING) EVER SOLD AT AUCTION

## $4.8 MILLION

Designed by Jean Louis, this sheer, nude, crystal-studded gown was reportedly so tight Marilyn had to be sewn into it. Worn during her famous performance for John F. Kennedy's 45th birthday celebrations in Madison Square Garden, New York, the original price tag was $1,440. It was previously auctioned in 1999 for $1.26 million.

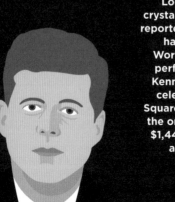

MARILYN

# THE SEVEN YEAR ITCH

WORN: SOLD:
1955 2011

MOST EXPENSIVE FILM COSTUME
EVER SOLD AT AUCTION

# $4.6 MILLION

This ivory cocktail dress with a plunging halter bodice was worn by Marilyn in *The Seven Year Itch* in one of Hollywood's most iconic fashion moments: "Ooh, do you feel the breeze from the subway?" she exclaims, as the wide skirt billows around her. The designer was William Travilla.

LEGACY

# CULTURAL ICON!

As one of the most famous women of the 20th century, since her death Marilyn has inspired countless homages and moved mountains of merchandise, continuing to be a constant presence throughout popular culture. Here are just a few examples of the ways in which she has been immortalized.

## ANDY WARHOL, MARILYN DIPTYCH, 1962

Many artists have made Marilyn their subject, but it is a series of silkscreen prints by Andy Warhol that are the most iconic works. Created in the weeks after her death in August 1962, and utilizing a publicity photograph from *Niagara,* Warhol repeats Marilyn's face 25 times in both colour and black and white in *Marilyn Diptych,* echoing the passing of a cultural legend.

## MAD ARCHITECTS, ABSOLUTE WORLD BUILDINGS, 2012

The taller of these two buildings – towering modern apartment blocks in Mississauga, Ontario, Canada – was nicknamed 'Marilyn Monroe' shortly after completion, due to its curvaceous forms.

**ELTON JOHN, 'CANDLE IN THE WIND', 1973**

A heartfelt tribute to the troubled star, Elton John's ballad includes the lyrics "Hollywood created a superstar / And pain was the price you paid." When it was updated and re-recorded in 1997 in memory of Princess Diana, it became the UK's best-selling single of all time.

# MADONNA, 'MATERIAL GIRL', 1985

Madonna's 1985 music video is a direct homage to Marilyn's rendition of 'Diamonds Are a Girl's Best Friend' from the film *Gentlemen Prefer Blondes*. Singers such as Beyoncé, Kylie Minogue and Christina Aguilera have also emulated the pink dress, sparkling jewels and attentive male dancers from the song.

# SGT. PEPPER'S LONELY HEARTS CLUB BAND, 1967

It's only fitting that one of the most famous album covers of all time, created by artist Peter Blake for one of the world's most famous bands, should feature Marilyn. She appears in the centre above Ringo Starr, flanked by writers William S. Burroughs and Edgar Allan Poe, explorer Dr David Livingstone and comedian Tommy Handley.

# CHANEL NO. 5

The French fashion house drew on Marilyn's claim that No. 5 was the only thing she wore to bed, using her image to advertise the perfume in 1994 and 2013. Marilyn has been used posthumously to promote many other brands, including American Airlines, Max Factor and Absolut Vodka.

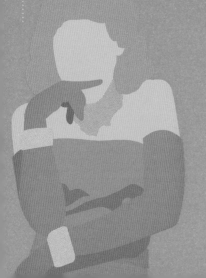

# TYPOGRAPHIC MARILYN

DRUGS MUSICAL SUBWAY STYLE CONSPIRACY SEX FOSTER HOMES

BLONDE 1950S 1926 LATENESS COLUMBIA

PIN-UP

MARILYN

BOMBSHELL CHILDHOOD HOLLYWOOD

SOME LIKE IT HOT ACTING GLAMOUR NORMA JEANE LOS ANGELES

JFK ORPHANAGE DIVORCE FASHION

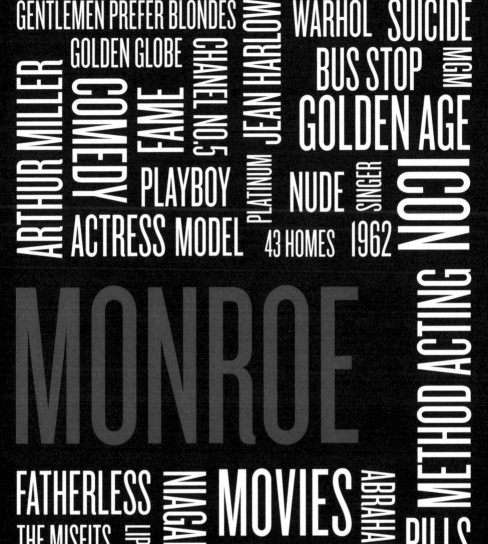

GENTLEMEN PREFER BLONDES

WARHOL  SUICIDE

GOLDEN GLOBE

BUS STOP

MGM

ARTHUR MILLER

COMEDY

FAME

CHANEL No.5

IML

PLATINUM  JEAN HARLOW

GOLDEN AGE

PLAYBOY

NUDE

SINGER

ICON

ACTRESS MODEL

43 HOMES  1962

MONROE

METHOD ACTING

FATHERLESS

NIAGARA

MOVIES

ABRAHAM LINCOLN

PILLS

THE MISFITS  LIPS

DEPRESSION

FOX  CINEMA

THE SEVEN YEAR ITCH

CHAMPAGNE

THREE HUSBANDS  LOVE

BEAUTY

JOE DIMAGGIO  HOW TO MARRY A MILLIONAIRE  MILITARY

LEGACY

# AWARDS!

Though she would never be nominated for an Oscar, Marilyn received a host of awards throughout her career, which trace her rise as a star.

 **1948**

**Artichoke Queen, town of Castroville, California**

**Miss Press Club, The Los Angeles Press Club**

 **1951**

**Best Young Box Office Personality, Henrietta Awards**

**The Girl Most Wanted to Examine, 7th Division Medical Corps**

**Miss Cheesecake of the Year, *Stars and Stripes* newspaper**

**The Present All GIs Would Like to Find in Their Christmas Stocking**

 **1952**

**Fastest Rising Star, Photoplay Awards**

New Faces Award, Detroit Free Press

**Most Promising Female Newcomer, *Look* magazine**

**Miss Cheesecake of the Year, *Stars and Stripes* newspaper**

**1953**

Most Popular Movie Actress, Independent Theatre Owners of Arkansas

**Best Young Box Office Personality, *Redbook* magazine**

**The Best Friend a Diamond Ever Had, The Jewelry Academy**

**1953**

Female World
Film Favourite,
Henrietta Awards

Most Popular
Female Star,
Photoplay
Awards

**1954**

Best Actress, for
*Gentlemen Prefer
Blondes* and *How
to Marry a Millionaire,*
Photoplay Awards

**US**

Recognition of Her
Unselfish Service
Rendered
to the Armed
Forces in Korea

**1956**

**NOMINATED**

**NOMINATED**

Best Foreign
Actress, for *The
Seven Year Itch,*
BAFTA Awards

Best Actress
in a Motion
Picture – Comedy
or Musical, for
*Bus Stop,* Golden
Globe Awards

**1958**

Best Foreign
Actress, for
*The Prince and
the Showgirl,*
David di Donatello
Awards (Italy)

**NOMINATED**

Best Foreign
Actress, for
*The Prince and
the Showgirl,*
BAFTA Awards

**1959**

Best Foreign
Actress, for
*The Prince and
the Showgirl,*
Crystal Star
Awards (France)

**1960**

Best Actress
in a Comedy or
Musical, for *Some
Like It Hot,* Golden
Globe Awards

**1962**

Female World
Film Favourite,
Henrietta Award,
Golden Globe Awards

# #METOO AND MARILYN

Sexual coercion has been endemic in Hollywood since the industry's inception. Efforts to call this out, such as the recent #MeToo campaign – which started in the wake of the scandal surrounding film producer Harvey Weinstein in 2017 – are nothing new either. In fact, Marilyn was an early whistleblower. At the age of 26, she went on the record for an article called 'Wolves I Have Known', which appeared in *Motion Picture and Television Magazine* in January 1953. Although she didn't actually name names, the article detailed her many experiences of fighting off unwanted male attention, and advised women on how to handle such situations.

"THEY SAY I'M WHISTLE BAIT. COULD BE, BUT I'M FOREVER MEETING GUYS WHO DON'T STOP AT A WHISTLE. I'VE LEARNED TO HANDLE THEM ALL."

# GENDER RATIOS IN HOLLYWOOD IN 2018

**MALE**

**FEMALE**

By standing up to her studio in protest against being typecast, Marilyn incited the wrath of her bosses, who led a campaign to tarnish her professional reputation. It failed, and when she announced the formation of Marilyn Monroe Productions in 1955, Marilyn became the first woman in Hollywood to have a majority share in a production company. Today, despite making up over half of cinema audiences in America, women continue to be under-represented in the business of making movies. In the top 100 highest-grossing US films of 2018, women accounted for:

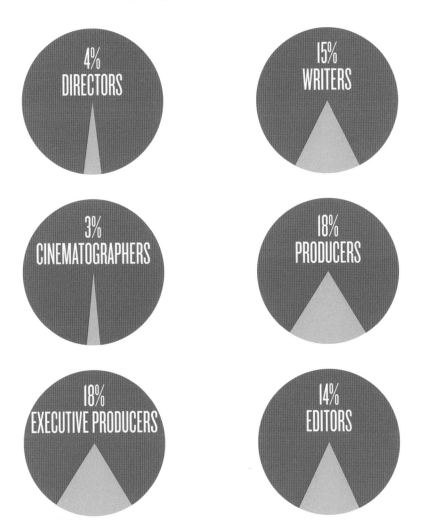

4%
DIRECTORS

15%
WRITERS

3%
CINEMATOGRAPHERS

18%
PRODUCERS

18%
EXECUTIVE PRODUCERS

14%
EDITORS

# BIOGRAPHIES

## Johnny Hyde
### (1896–1950)
Hyde was Marilyn's agent and 'sugar daddy' during her early movie career, and he was fundamental in helping her reach the big time. He fell deeply in love with the young starlet, though Marilyn refused his marriage proposal.

## Dr. Ralph Greenson
### (1910–79)
Marilyn's psychiatrist during the last year of her life, Greenson also treated many other Hollywood stars. She began seeing him daily and became a surrogate member of the family. The level of his control over her life has attracted many critics.

## Arthur Miller
### (1915–2005)
Marilyn first met prominent playwright Miller in 1951, but they would not meet again until 1955. They married in 1956, which helped Marilyn to establish a new image as a serious actress, but their marriage finally broke down on the set of *The Misfits* in 1960.

## Milton Greene
### (1922–85)
An eminent fashion photographer, Greene became close friends with Marilyn after a 1953 photoshoot. Along with his wife Amy, Greene supported Marilyn during her battle with Fox. He co-owned and ran the business side of Marilyn Monroe Productions.

## Lee Strasberg
### (1901–82)
Strasberg became a prominent mentor and father figure to Marilyn following her move to New York in 1955. As director of the Actors Studio, he coached many of the leading screen stars of the 20th century.

## Sidney Skolsky
### (1905–83)
A close friend and ally, Skolsky was a renowned Hollywood columnist who championed Marilyn's talents after they met in the late 1940s. The two had been planning a biopic of Jean Harlow when Marilyn died.

**Joe DiMaggio (1914–99)**
Major league baseball player for the New York Yankees, DiMaggio became Marilyn's second husband in 1954. Their marriage was volatile and lasted only 9 months, though Joe remained a loyal friend and a reunion was rumoured at the time of her death.

**John F. Kennedy (1917–63)**
Speculation surrounds a possible relationship between the 35th President of the United States and Marilyn, and his implication in her death. Accounts of some of Marilyn's friends suggest they spent a night together, but only four meetings have been documented.

**Robert Kennedy (1925-68)**
The US Attorney General from 1961-1963, Bobby Kennedy met Marilyn in 1961 and they became friends, speaking regularly on the phone. Rumours of an affair, and speculation over his involvement in her death, have never produced conclusive evidence.

**Dr. Marianne Kris (1900-80)**
From 1955 until 1961, Marilyn was a patient of Kris, a Vienna-born psychoanalyst who studied under Sigmund Freud. Their relationship ended after Marilyn endured a traumatic stay on a locked psychiatric ward, following her doctor's recommendation.

**Paula Strasberg (1911–66)**
As Marilyn's personal acting coach and confidante, Strasberg (wife of Lee) worked on the set of all her films from *Bus Stop,* in 1956, onwards. She became the key emotional and professional support in Marilyn's life.

**Natasha Lytess (1913–64)**
Marilyn met acting coach Lytess during a short contract with Columbia Pictures in 1948. The two developed an intense seven-year working relationship and friendship, which ended when Marilyn started dating Joe DiMaggio.

working relationship

husband

friend

psychiatrist

# INDEX